HIDING

by Karen Wallace and Charles Fuge

W

FRANKLIN WATTS

LONDON • SYDNEY

All animals hide.
They change their colour.
They change their shape.
They pretend to be
something else.
These ways of
hiding are called
camouflage.

A horned frog who looks just like a leaf will be safe in the forest.

You can discover the secrets of camouflage. Some of them are hidden in this book!

A speckled coat hides this baby deer in shadowy woodland.

This stone fish rests among stones but his poisonous spine keeps his enemies away.

Animals hide
so they can attack
without being seen.

WATCH
OUT
for this
tiger!

Do you think this crocodile
looks like a log?

4

A polar bear hides her black nose so she is almost invisible against the snow.

A sloth's fur is covered in lichen and moss. She is as green as the tree she lives in.

6

Animals use their colour to
hide from their enemies.

A tawny frogmouth
closes his eyes
and pretends
he's a branch.

And this caterpillar
looks like a bit of twig.

Some African butterflies
hide by living in clusters.
Some of them taste nasty.

Some of them don't.
But a hungry bird
doesn't like to risk
making a mistake!

9

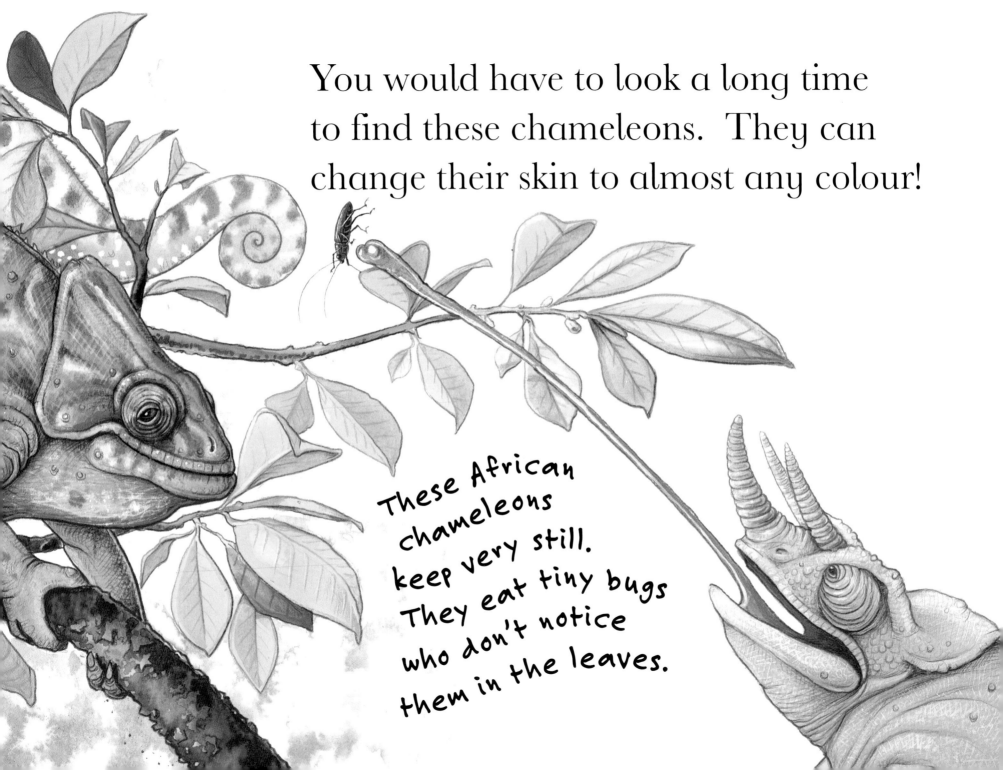

You would have to look a long time
to find these chameleons. They can
change their skin to almost any colour!

These African
chameleons
keep very still.
They eat tiny bugs
who don't notice
them in the leaves.

Eyes can give the game away!
Hide them and no-one
will eat you!

An angel fish and
a butterfly fish hide their
eyes behind a black stripe.

When a raccoon prowls
at night, he doesn't
want anyone
to see him.

12

Eyes can protect you if you have fierce pretend ones.

KEEP AWAY!
This frog's bottom is watching you!

Some animals decorate themselves so nobody knows they are there.

An African bug covers itself in ant bodies so it doesn't look tasty to its enemies.

Many animals pretend they are plants so they can hide and stay safe.

This leaf insect sways like a leaf. Could you tell the difference?

Who wants to eat thorns? These thorn bugs can fool a hungry bird.

An Australian leafy seadragon looks
like a piece of seaweed. You'd have
to look carefully
to see him.

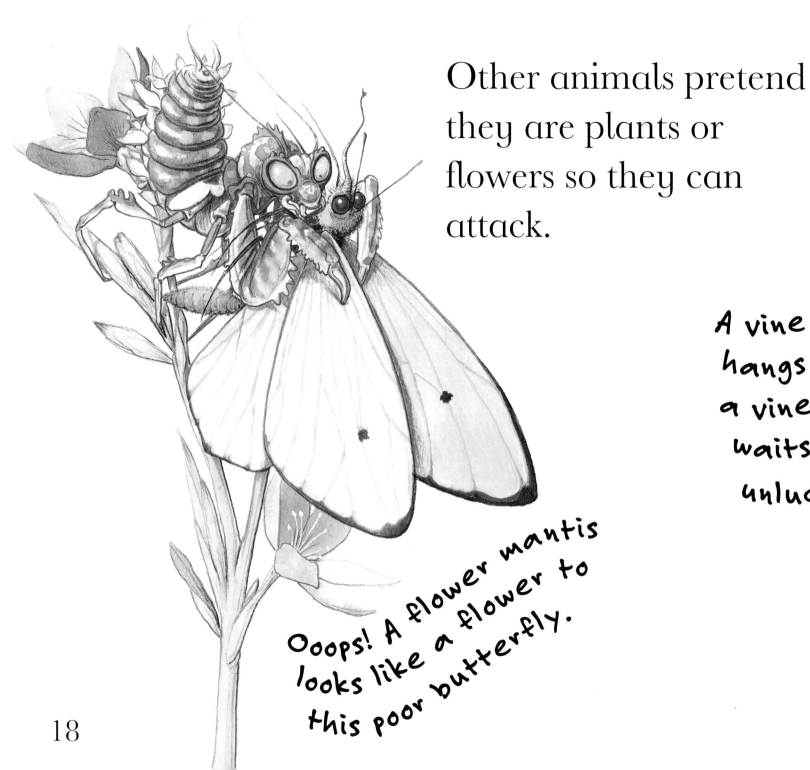

Other animals pretend they are plants or flowers so they can attack.

A vine snake hangs like a vine and waits for an unlucky bird.

Ooops! A flower mantis looks like a flower to this poor butterfly.

This African spider pretends he's just a thorn.

A hungry leaf fish pretends he is a leaf drifting through the water.

19

Sometimes harmless insects look like harmful ones so their enemies won't eat them.

Each one is pretending to be a wasp, a hornet or an ant with a nasty sting.

20

This harmless Malaysian keelback flattens his neck and pretends to be a deadly snake like a cobra.

Nobody wants to eat you if they think you are dead already!

An opossum pretends to be dead because most of its enemies don't eat dead animals.

22

A grass snake rolls on its belly and lets its mouth hang open.

If you were a bird would you eat this click beetle?

23

Birds lay specially coloured eggs so their enemies won't see them.

Can you see this little tern's eggs?

Dogfish egg sacs are called mermaids' purses. They look just like seaweed.

24

This mother cuckoo has stolen a reed warbler's egg and laid her own in its place.

Can you spot the cuckoo's egg? This reed warbler can't.

25

Some baby animals have special colours to keep them safe from their enemies.

A stripey coat helps wild boar piglets blend in with the shadows.

When a young zebra stays close to his mother he is almost impossible to see.

A harp seal pup is white as the snow around him.

27

All animals hide.
Who is hiding here?

More information

Angel fish – the black pretend eye on the fish's back is there to trick enemies and draw attention away from its head (page 12).

Baby deer – as it grows bigger and stronger the coat loses its speckles (page 3).

Chameleon – a chameleon flicks out a long sticky tongue to catch unlucky flies (page 10-11).

Crocodile – a crocodile can wait without moving for a long time. This helps him to trick other animals (page 4-5).

Cuckoo – the cuckoo lays one egg at a time in different birds' nests. The egg is slightly larger but looks like the other eggs (page 25).

Harp seal pup – when a pup is old enough to swim he loses his white coat and turns a mottled grey (page 27).

Hermit crab – this crab lives in many different sorts of shells. As it grows bigger it simply moves "house" (page 14).

Leafy sea-dragon – he is a kind of seahorse. He looks so much like a piece of floating seaweed that small fish hide behind him (page 17).

Opossum – playing dead does not keep it safe from all animals (page 22). Hyenas and vultures like to eat dead things. They are called scavengers.

Raccoon – a raccoon is a nocturnal animal which means it is active at night and rests during the day (page 12).

Vine snake – it kills its prey by injecting a small amount of poison from its fangs at the back of its mouth (page 18-19).

To Miranda

This edition 2004

First published by Franklin Watts
338 Euston Road, London, NW1 3BH

Franklin Watts Australia
Level 17/207 Kent Street, Sydney, NSW 2000

Series editor: Paula Borton
Art director: Robert Walster
Consultant: Dr Jim Flegg, Institute of Horticultural Research

Printed in Singapore

A CIP catalogue record is available from the British Library

ISBN 978 0 7496 5861 8

Franklin Watts is a division of Hachette Children's Books,
an Hachette Livre UK company.